WILD ONES

KANGAROOS

by
JILL
ANDERSON

NorthWord
Minnetonka, Minnesota

A strange-looking animal leaps and bounds through the grasslands and forests of Australia.

What is it?

It's a gray kangaroo!

But wait...

It's really **two** kangaroos!

A baby, called a joey, is going for a bouncy ride in its mother's furry pouch.

Red and gray kangaroos are the two biggest and most common kinds of kangaroos.

Their relatives include tree kangaroos, wallabies, and rat kangaroos.

Every kangaroo is built to be a champion hopper.

Its back legs are strong and
bendy. When it hops,
it pushes off with both feet
and springs forward.
Its heavy tail helps it balance.

A newborn joey has a lot of growing to do before it can hop like that.

It is not much bigger than a jellybean. The joey climbs into its mother's pouch and begins to drink her milk. It doesn't let go for four months!

When the joey is finally old enough to spend time out of the pouch, it stays close to its mother. At the first sign of danger, it **dives** back in— **headfirst!**

The mother kangaroo shows her joey how to find food and water. She and her baby play games that help it learn to protect itself. Before these lessons are done, she will be nursing a new joey.

In the evening and early morning, kangaroo families meet up with others nearby. They say **hello** by touching noses. Adult males come and go.

Together, the kangaroos feed
on grass and other plants.
They help each other listen and
watch for danger.

If one of them thumps its foot in warning, the whole group bounds away.

The midday sun
is very hot. Quietly,
each family hops away
to find a shady spot.

The joeys may get
a bath from mom
before they drift
off to sleep.

As the sun sets, the furry family stirs.

Then off they go again to join their friends in a grassy feast.

*For a most loving and
attentive mother
of the human kind: mine.*

—J. A.

Composed in the United States of America
Designed by Lois A. Rainwater • Edited by Kristen McCurry

Text © 2006 by Jill Anderson

NORTHWORD

Books for Young Readers
11571 K-Tel Drive
Minnetonka, MN 55343
www.tnkidsbooks.com

Photographs © 2006 provided by:
Frans Lanting/Minden Pictures: cover, pp. 2-3, 4-5, 17, 18-19; John McCann/istockphoto.com: back cover, p. 24;
Digital Vision/Punchstock.com: pp. 1, 7 (wallaby), 9, 15, 20; Mitsuaki Iwago/Minden Pictures: pp. 6, 8, 10-11, 16-17, 22-23;
Gerry Ellis/Minden Pictures: p. 7 (tree kangaroo); Mike Hill/Alamy Images: p. 7 (rat kangaroo);
Photodisc/Punchstock.com: p. 12; Jin Young Lee/istockphoto.com: p. 13; Danita Delimont/Alamy Images: p. 21.

Library of Congress Cataloging-in-Publication Data

Anderson, Jill.
Kangaroos / by Jill Anderson.
p. cm. -- (Wild ones)
ISBN 1-55971-935-4 (hardcover) -- ISBN 1-55971-936-2 (softcover)
1. Kangaroos--Juvenile literature. I. Title.

QL737.M35A53 2006

599.2'22--dc22   2005020871

Printed in Singapore
10 9 8 7 6 5 4 3 2 1